Mindfulness

A Practical Guide on How Mindfulness Can Stop Depression and Find Inner Peace

(Steps to Becoming More Present Through Mindfulness Meditation)

Adam Jones

Published by Rob Miles

© **Adam Jones**

All Rights Reserved

Mindfulness: A Practical Guide on How Mindfulness Can Stop Depression and Find Inner Peace (Steps to Becoming More Present Through Mindfulness Meditation)

ISBN 978-1-989990-78-0

All rights reserved. No part of this guide may be reproduced in any form without permission in writing from the publisher except in the case of brief quotations embodied in critical articles or reviews.

Legal & Disclaimer

The information contained in this book is not designed to replace or take the place of any form of medicine or professional medical advice. The information in this book has been provided for educational and entertainment purposes only.

The information contained in this book has been compiled from sources deemed reliable, and it is accurate to the best of the Author's knowledge; however, the Author cannot guarantee its accuracy and validity and cannot be held liable for any errors or omissions. Changes are periodically made to this book. You must consult your doctor or get professional medical advice before using any of the suggested remedies, techniques, or information in this book.

Upon using the information contained in this book, you agree to hold harmless the Author from and against any damages, costs, and expenses, including any legal fees potentially resulting from the application of any of the information provided by this guide. This disclaimer applies to any damages or injury caused by the use and application, whether directly or indirectly, of any advice or information presented, whether for breach of contract, tort, negligence, personal injury, criminal intent, or under any other cause of action.

You agree to accept all risks of using the information presented inside this book. You need to consult a professional medical practitioner in order to ensure you are both able and healthy enough to participate in this program.

Table of Contents

INTRODUCTION 1

CHAPTER 1: WHAT IS MINDFULNESS? 9

CHAPTER 2: ALLEVIATING STRESS WITH MINDFULNESS .. 25

CHAPTER 3: MINDFULNESS IS... 31

CHAPTER 4: HOW THE EGO OPERATES 37

CHAPTER 5: BECOMING MORE MINDFUL EVERYDAY 44

CHAPTER 6: TAKING THE MYSTERY OUT OF MEDITATION 55

CHAPTER 7: UNDERSTANDING MINDFULNESS MEDITATION 67

CHAPTER 8: WHAT IS MINDFULNESS? 76

CHAPTER 9: REAL WORLD MINDFULNESS 81

CHAPTER 10: PUTTING MINDFULNESS MEDITATION INTO PRACTICE 88

CHAPTER 11: POSITIVE IMPACTS 105

CHAPTER 12: A FEW MORE MINDFULNESS PRACTICES .. 120

CHAPTER 13: THE BASICS OF MINDFUL LIVING 125

CHAPTER 14: COMPASSION FOR SELF 134

CHAPTER 15: MINDFULNESS FOR BEGINNERS 156

CHAPTER 16: LIVING IN THE PRESENT AND ACCEPTING LIFE CHALLENGES 173

CONCLUSION 183

Introduction

We live in a time that is unprecedented in human history. Our standard of living today would be considered science fiction or fantasy fifty years ago. We have 24-hour media cycles, high-speed internet, quantum physics, GPS, and other technologies that offer us greater opportunity for enhancing our lives as never before. Despite all these advances, the level of our collective happiness, fulfillment, and wisdom has not kept pace. For all our advances, we have not invested the same kind of determination to understand the nature of who we are. We have forgotten who we are at an essential level of our being and that amnesia is preventing our innate wisdom from shining through. This wisdom is being eclipsed by our undisciplined mind. We live out our lives with an endless parade of thoughts passing through our consciousness, many of which preoccupy our attention. The purpose of mindfulness is to transcend our thoughts by disciplining our mind.

Think about your life. What is happening in your life that is preventing you from experiencing inner peace or equanimity? What is preventing you from experiencing true happiness, a happiness that is independent of other people, situations, or events? We so often believe that happiness or inner peace is contingent upon us getting some result in our lives. That result we are looking for may be a healed relationship or freedom from an existing relationship. The result that we are looking for may be overcoming our thoughts of the past or the forgiveness of ourselves or others. Perhaps what we are looking for is overcoming financial hardship or physical illness.

Regardless of what we are looking for, it will not lead to true happiness. If we fail to achieve the result that we are looking for, we will either become disenchanted, disappointed, or continue to strive for that which we are looking for. If we achieve the result that we worked for, we may enjoy the feeling of happiness and success, but it will only be temporary. With time, our sense of victory will diminish, and we will start the cycle anew. In this way, we are like hamsters on a wheel. No matter how much energy we put into our effort, we often find ourselves back where we started.

Take a moment and think about your life. On a scale of 0-10, how fulfilled are you? Do you have a sense that something is missing? Do you feel as though your life is somehow incomplete? If you were honest with yourself when answering these questions, most likely you did not rate your sense of fulfillment as a ten. Also, you most likely admitted that there is something missing from your life, which is preventing you from experiencing complete fulfillment. If you are among the few who rated your fulfillment as a 10, and you experience a sense of wholeness in your life, how stable is this feeling? Do you feel this way some of the time, or most of the time? If you can sincerely say that you feel a sense of wholeness and fulfillment most of the time, this book may provide you with additional insights and nuggets of wisdom to enhance your life even more. If you are like the majority of the human race, this book offers you an opportunity to experience your life at a level which is beyond your mind's ability to comprehend.

To live a life where we experience a sense of wholeness within our being and to experience a sense of inner peace and oneness with life, is to experience our individual life, merged with life itself. Let me rephrase this, as my last statement is incorrect. To live a life where we experience a sense of wholeness within our being, to experience a sense of inner peace and oneness with life, is to break the spell that has led us to believe that our individual life is separate from the rest of the world and the return to the realization that our individual life is inseparable from life itself. In other words, **You are Life!** What you have just read may seem abstract rather than relevant. It may seem more like prose or lofty thinking rather than being realistic. If this is true, I cannot blame you, as I have had the same reaction 20 years ago.

There is a story about a man who was walking along the side of a road. Out from a distance, he sees a horse and rider approaching him. As the rider approaches the man, the man can see that the rider is unable to control his horse. The rider is desperately trying to hold on as the horse gallops full speed. When the rider is close enough, the man recognizes the rider; it was his friend. The man shouts out to the rider: "Where are you going?" The rider replies: "I do not know. Ask the horse." This story is a metaphor for our lives. The rider is the metaphor for you and me. The horse is a metaphor for our minds. Most of us are like the rider as we have lost control of our lives. We have lost control of our lives because we have delegated our experience of life to the whims of our minds. Just as the rider, we have allowed our minds to determine where we are going. Because we allow our minds to dictate our experiences of life, we do not feel whole; this is why we feel like something is missing. As long as we turn to our minds for directions, we will not gain clarity and realize the truth of who we are. To experience profound happiness, peace, and freedom requires that we regain control of our horse. Instead of following the dictates of our minds, we need to take charge of our minds.

To practice mindfulness is to be awakened from an ancient dream and come to know that we can experience absolute freedom, happiness, and well-being. More importantly, we can make a difference in the lives of others. If enough of us learn mindfulness, we can change the future of thisplanet.

Mindfulness is not a form of spiritual thought, nor does it involve adopting a belief system. In fact, practicing mindfulness is inaccurate as to practice mindfulness implies that there is something to practice. Rather, mindfulness means taking the time to notice what exist already. My hope is that you will approach this book with an open mind, an open heart, and the courage to challenge the beliefs that you hold for yourself and others. If you persist in exploring mindfulness, you will experience your life in a whole new fulfilling and amazing way.

Chapter 1: What Is Mindfulness?

The question this chapter is built around is by no means easy to answer even though it deals with a somewhat fascinating and comprehensible topic. A lot of attempts have been made to define mindfulness, even in dictionaries. For example, a dictionary defines mindfulness as "stress-reduction training: a program designed to reduce the psychological and physical effects of stress that involves meditation, yoga, and other relaxation methods."

Some dictionaries have defined it the same way but in somewhat different words; others have conjured up entirely different images while defining it. A few dictionaries have actually equated it with meditation.

Leave it to the dictionaries to define mindfulness differently because it's familiar to us. Whether we call it so or not, each of us does it with a different approach and frequency. However, mindfulness is not a subject to be explained in grammatical terms. It is a process, a practice, a therapy, and a study of how to bring one's attention to the experiences of one's present moment; this can be cultivated by practicing meditation and engaging in different forms of training.

From all of the above, you can see that mindfulness is a basic human ability; it's what we are able to do if we truly want to, it's a skill we naturally possess. It is the ability to be consciously present and be fully aware of where you are, what you're doing, and what's happening around you, without being overly responsive or overwhelmed. With the habit of daily practice, mindfulness is readily available to us. The definitions might be varied because mindfulness takes many shapes and it goes by many names.

Don't we all have the capacity to be fully present? Then we don't have to change who or what we are to be mindful. All you have to do if you want to benefit from mindfulness is to cultivate your inherent qualities and tendencies to be mindful. How? With simple regimented practices that have been scientifically proven to be of great benefit to our well-being. Simply put, that which helps us separate ourselves from our reactions, that which breaks down our impulsive responses is mindfulness.

Unlike what is conjured up in bizarre definitions, it is not required that you have a meditation bench, or couch, or any special equipment for that matter. Everything you need in order to be able to bring out the mindfulness skills in you is time and space.

Viewing it from a spiritual angle, it becomes simpler. The word "mindfulness" is translated from a term taken from Pali, an ancient Indo-European language, now spoken in India, but formerly spoken in South Asia. The word is "sati." It is a significant element of Sanskrit and it's found in Buddhist scriptures.

Schools, hospitals, prisons, foster care homes for the elderly, orphanages, correctional facilities, and other centers have incorporated Jon Kabat Zinn's model of mindfulness into their programs. They are witnessing tremendous success with regards to rehabilitation, healthy aging, excellence in athletics, and management of kids with special needs, as well as mediating the period of perinatal.

To help develop mindful meditation, a lot of exercises have been designed, though they are not a must, as explained earlier. You can achieve this by sitting on a chair with a straight back or sitting on the floor or on a cushion with your legs crossed and your eyes closed, focusing your attention on the sensations you experience when breathing and on the movements in your abdomen.

Another mind meditation exercise is body scan meditation. Here you focus on different areas of the body and observe the sensations of the present moments. You could also take note of the sounds, perceptions, thoughts, feelings, and actions of the present moment.

You can begin any of these exercises with a short period of daily meditation, say 10 minutes per day. With regular practice and time, you will find it easier to develop mindfulness, and with a lengthier duration.

Anyone, regardless of age, physical disability, religion, or any other social factor, can engage in the practice of mindfulness and be successful. There are absolutely no barriers to it.

Why do people need to be mindful?

People, even you, need to be mindful. Do you know that if you are not aware of your immediate environment, circumstances and sounds that surround you, you might end up hurting not only others, but also yourself? The definition of mindfulness we earlier discussed shows why we need to mindful.

Let's quickly point out at this stage that mindfulness shouldn't be confused with alertness. While alertness deals with your state of mind or mental content, (whether helpful or harmful), mindfulness is a controlled and conscious awareness of all the contents of your mind.

Now, let's focus more specifically on the reasons why people need to be mindful.

It Helps Manage Stress

A survey conducted by the American Psychological Association in 2015 indicates that, every year, the stress level is increasing all around the world. About one-quarter of Americans are reported to be facing "extreme stress" while one-third said that their stress level has upped in the last 12 months. The same survey says that four in every five adults are experiencing at least one of the physical symptoms of stress.

Unfortunately, most of us are not good at coping with stress because we're not taught the skills to do so. Those who engage in stress management activities do so less often than ideally. There are some who imbibe the practices of exercising and hanging out with loved ones, while others engage in unhealthy habits like overeating and excessive use of the Internet and television.

However, learning to be mindful comes with engaging in appropriate physical activities like taking a deep breath, making gentle movements, and assuming an easeful posture that soothes the body's nerves. These are the cognitive strategies for taking care of what life demands from us. After 40 years of ongoing research about the relationship between stress and mindfulness, it has been discovered that among other things, people practicing mindfulness will have lower stress levels and reduced risk of depression and anxiety.

As far back as the late 70s, the University of Massachusetts has also campaigned for what doctors, therapists, politicians, and educators are propagating today. All indices point to the fact that the continued practice of mindfulness will alter the way we handle distressing emotions. Since we all know that stress shoots up blood pressure and weakens body's immune system, lowering the quality of our sleep, we need mindfulness to take care of the stress in our lives.

It Helps Us To Improve Relationships

When we're mindfully present in our interactions with our friends, acquaintances, and relations, what we see in them is beyond the obvious. When we're able to see past their present failings and errors and see their potential, we are more likely to accept them for who they are. Since we've seen the good in them, together with their hidden talents and skills, it will be easier for us to accept them without any kind of judgment, and we'll even respect them. This is a kind of encouragement for the recipients of our admiration to progress. It, in turn, boosts their self-esteem without flattery.

Similarly, because we're absorbed in the present moment, those we are with at that moment usually notice it and are happy that we're with them wholly. Our practice of mindfulness thus fosters hearty interactions. In the middle of a conversation, when people ask, "Are you with me?" it indicates they feel uncomfortable with the person they're conversing with, and that stifles interaction. But some have learned that mindfulness attracts people to themselves because they will like to be with those who will give them their time and undivided attention. In this way, mindfulness helps to improve a relationship.

People Are Distracted

It's very difficult for people to relate to their current moment because there are just too many distractions than we can't cope with. For instance, if you ask people to state what they are doing at the moment and what they are thinking about, you'll realize that what they are doing is quite different from what they are thinking about. So they're not in their present moment. Thanks to distractions, a wandering mind leads people to make careless and costly mistakes. For example, it results in time-wasting and loss of productivity when objects are misplaced due to lack of mindfulness.

Mindfulness makes it possible to have a heightened awareness of what we're doing at the moment. Bringing us back to the moment and helping us remain there, mindfulness will help us to combat distractions that would have prevented us from savoring the moments around us. We will thus be able to admire the beauty of nature in something as common as a blue sky, flying birds, color, aroma, depth, height, flora and fauna, and even in the nuances of the languages we speak. When we're no longer distracted, our appreciation for our environment increases.

It Helps People To Kick-Start Self Reflection

When you're wholly present somewhere in a particular time and place, you'll be able to savor the sweetness and the otherwise evanescent essence of moments. Then you'll be in a better position to compare the moment with past interactions. By successfully doing so, you can better galvanize your life for a better future.

Top 5 Mindfulness Practices

Now that you know the benefits you can derive from mindfulness, aren't you feeling like getting started right away? No, not before you're thoroughly familiar with the top mindfulness practices. Let's now do justice to the top five of them, in no particular order.

Get an early start of your day

This does not mean that you have to rush things over. Let your day begin slowly, before sunrise, so that you can enjoy it as the sun is rising, while sipping a cup of tea. Free yourself of all those distracting gadgets. Don't forget, you've got a hectic day ahead. So try to practice mindfulness quite early in the day.

Relish the pleasantness of your breakfast

In addition to avoiding a rushed start of your day, resist the urge to gallop through your meal, especially your breakfast, if you really want to practice mindfulness. Don't think you can just gulp down whatever is in the bowl or quickly devour that food over the sink and drop the dish. No, that's not a breakfast for someone with mindful habits. Rather, sit and relax at the dining table and concentrate on what you're enjoying-your warm meal. Mind the design on the plate and appreciate the taste with each bite you take. By so doing, you're practicing mindfulness.

Individualize people

Treat each person you meet as an individual. As you go to work, don't be in a haste so as to ignore people you meet. There's a huge difference between a casual greet and an exchange of pleasantries. Don't just say a quick "hello".

Complement it with a friendly smile. Gaze into the eyes of everyone that deserve your greetings. Ask about things that should be important to them, like family, free time, and weekend activities.

Plan Ahead Your Affairs

Design a To-Do list and keep to it. Fill the early part of your day with the most important tasks first, and fill the latter part of the day with smaller and less important ones. As you plan your days and the activities scheduled for each day, factor in some 5-10-minute walks intermittently throughout the day. Also, remember to take 2-minute breaks from your workstation every 30 minutes, to stand or stretch your legs, arms, and back.

Maintain an open-door policy

Shun the practice of working behind a closed door. Keep your door wide open.

Give yourself the opportunity to hear the sounds outside your office. Try and figure out the rhythms and occurrences of each day. Differentiate between the sound of harmony and the sound of chaos, as well as the sound in-between. And if you're not working in a closed-door office, you'll be able to see the movements around you and hear the sounds better. Being mindful requires that you don't consider these as disruptive. Consider them as the sound of fellow workers working around the office.

The above tips are the top five of innumerable ones that can help you benefit from mindfulness.

Chapter 2: Alleviating Stress With Mindfulness

When stress overwhelms you, every part of your body is affected. Your muscles tense. Your heart beats faster. You perspire more. On top of it all, the flood of adrenaline and stress hormones like cortisol diminishes your ability to think clearly.

Mindfulness exercises train an individual to focus their attention to the physical and emotional feelings they are experiencing in the present moment. While it seems odd, the stress you are feeling is something you need to feel in order to control it.

Military training is conducted in extreme situations to amplify the stress soldiers feel. Part of the discipline they learn is focused on controlling stress in the moment. It's not mindfulness, but it illustrates how we can only learn to master our feelings of stress by sitting with our stress.

Most people instinctively distract themselves from stress because the sensations are more than they wish to bear. As a result, when stress arises again they are ill-prepared to cope. So the first thing we will learn about in alleviating stress with mindfulness is the art of sitting with the stress you are feeling.

This is counter to our instincts. Stress produces a fight or flight response. As the adrenaline surges through our bodies we seek to either fight the stress or run from it. Mindfulness recommends a third way. Embrace your stress and understand it. Be aware of it in the moment.

To best accomplish that, advocates of mindfulness have prescribed a means of attaining the mental capacity to sit with our stress. These mindfulness exercises all focus on the goal of awareness. In particular mindfulness exercises encourage a feeling of non-judgmental awareness. Do not judge your feelings. Observe them and accept them.

Distractions must be avoided as you seek to be more mindful of your feelings and the moment. In modern times, distractions are always present. Those distractions will prevent you from focusing on awareness. So the first step we will take to alleviate stress will be to block out distractions. This involves turning off your phone, stepping away from your desk and getting away from the things that will commonly distract you. Co-workers count, too.

One of the best ways you can do that is to go for a quick walk. Leave your phone behind if you'd like. If the weather is pleasant go outside and take a walk around the building or parking lot. As you walk, slow your thinking. This short diversion from your work allows you an uninterrupted opportunity to consider what caused you to feel stressed.

Do you remember the supervisor that stressed me out? I began coping with that stress by taking a walk after any encounter that provoked a feeling of distress. As I'd walk I'd think about what was said to me and really analyzed what I was being asked. I discovered the words being used were often neutral. It was just his aggressive tone and posture that got me stressed.

With this knowledge, I could begin to slow down conversations with my supervisor.

Instead of lurching for a defensive response because I was stressed, I heard more of what was being asked of me. And I calmly responded. It wasn't easy - certainly not at first. But as I continued to go for walks, my response improved.

Another tactic I used, when a walk was either impossible or very inconvenient was to take five minutes at my desk. I would position certain pictures I had taken on the walls of my cubicle. To the right of my monitor was a photograph of the Lone Cypress in Pebble Beach, California. To the left was a hawk I had photographed in flight to the west of Golden Gate Park in San Francisco. Another picture I hung up was of Seven Falls in Colorado.

Whenever stress set in and I needed to break from it, I'd look at these scenic pictures and let my mind go there. I'd shut out interruptions and think about the smell of the air, the sounds of cars going by as I stood and snapped a picture of these scenic landmarks. As I soothed myself, I would think about the stress I was feeling and then why I was feeling the stress. I would think about the pace of my heartbeat and why my mind had been racing. And within five minutes I no longer felt stressed.

Chapter 3: Mindfulness Is…

Prior to us really digging deep into practical practices and tools that you can use to begin implementing mindfulness into your own life, it is crucial that we develop a clear understanding of what mindfulness truly is. This will allow us to get on the same page and work from a similar angle so that you truly can make the most of your own mindfulness practice.

Mindfulness is a tool, a technique, and a way of life. It is much more powerful than most people actually realize, and it can also be much more intimidating. Recognizing that mindfulness is a tool that we can use to shape and create our own lives is exciting, empowering, and inspiring. But it can also lead to us feeling defensive and perhaps a little uncomfortable. After all, admitting that we have had the power the entire time may feel as though we are admitting that we had failed ourselves in the past, at times when we were not in a state of peace or joy. This is where mindfulness can become slightly intimidating.

Taking the power of your own life into your own hands is a major task to undertake, and it is also highly crucial if you want to live your dream life. Still, it is important to understand that it is not always the easiest task, particularly in the beginning. Until you really develop an understanding of this power and how it contributes to your way of life and develop a synergy with this power, mindfulness may feel uncomfortable or even burdensome. Sometimes, it may feel **easier** to live on autopilot or in a state of survival mode. After all, then you don't actually have to slow down and ask yourself sensitive questions, like: "How do I **really** feel about this?" "Why am I unhappy right now?" "What is causing me to lead a life that lacks peace?"

Although mindfulness can seem intimidating and the process of taking responsibility for and control over your own life can be somewhat challenging, it is important to realize that this challenge is definitely one that you can undertake **and succeed at.** Each and every single individual who decides that they want to change their lives through mindfulness has the choice to make that a successful change. As soon as you determine that you are going to take control and that you want to be in the driver's seat of your own experience, you are no longer bound by someone else's rules, expectations, or other requirements of you. Instead, you hold the power to say important things like: "No." "That doesn't make me feel good." "You are not respecting my boundaries." And other statements that protect our personal space, peace, joy, and happiness.

When you truly make the decision to commit to mindfulness, and you become stubborn in your desire to uphold that commitment, you immediately set the tone for your entire life to change. You empower yourself to take on a role of leadership in your own life, and you give yourself permission to be responsible for creating your own reality. You give yourself the keys and the answer to changing things you dislike, honoring who you truly are, and creating a reality that fuels you and inspires you. This is all a valuable part of creating the type of life that allows you to enjoy peace, joy, happiness, and positivity.

So, now that you understand what mindfulness allows you to do and have an honest understanding of what it may feel like in the early stages, it's time to understand what mindfulness truly is. Are you ready? It's simple, really.

Mindfulness is defined by the dictionary as "the quality or state of being conscious or aware of something," and "a mental state achieved by focusing one's awareness on the present moment, while calmly acknowledging and accepting one's feelings, thoughts, and bodily sensations. Used as a therapeutic technique."

Mindfulness is the attention you give to yourself, your thoughts, your needs, your reality, your preferences, your likes, your dislikes, your body, and your**self.** It is a series of both mental and physical practices that allow you to slow down, become aware of who you are and what you are, and truly assess all areas of your life. On a grand scale, mindfulness is the practice of understanding and allowing peace, joy, and happiness into your life. On a day-to-day scale, it is a series of tools such as meditation, self-awareness, and other techniques that allow you to become mindfulness over your sense of self, your body, your emotions, and your life.

In essence, mindfulness is the key to everything involving joy, peace, happiness, serenity, love, passion, and **true living.**

Chapter 4: How The Ego Operates

Let me begin this by chapter by pointing out that it's my belief that everyone has an ego. No matter how enlightened a person is, we all have an ego. The difference, however, is that some people are aware of the ego and thereby have control over how much pain it will inflict on them. Some people might have an ego that has been resting for years. But when something comes up, it could be something that identifies them with an experience in their youth, their ego takes over. One of the biggest loopholes that the ego will take advantage of is going in through the backdoor. This means, when a person reaches some form of enlightenment or awareness, they could find themselves thinking something along the lines of "look at all these other people, they are so stuck in their ego". Of course this is the ego talking. In this case, the ego wants to be better or one step higher than others. The reason why I wanted to bring up the ego so early in the book is because he is the biggest enemy when trying to live in the present moment.

The Need for Identification

Think of a small child, it's being placed on this world with an enormous amount of curiosity. You can see in their eyes that they are experiencing life to the fullest. Their senses are always alert and the present moment is the only thing that matters to them. Fast forward 12 years and the same child will have gone through some changes that are now causing it to suffer more. One of these changes are the discoveries of the words "I" and "my/mine". When the child experiences strong identification with things, what happens when their bike gets stolen, for example? They will identify with the bike and say something along the lines of: "My bike got stolen" or "I lost my bike". Can you see how the identification with "My" and "I" is causing unnecessary suffering? Had it been their brothers bike, who they got the same use from, do you think they would have got the same pain? Simply because it was "their" bike the pain gets amplified. It's like a part of them was broken when the bike disappeared.

Now think of your own life, are there any identification that is causing unnecessary pain in your life? Do you sometimes amplify the pain by using the words "I" and "my/mine"? Think back of a time when you've lost something, it could be a partner, friend, or a thing that you've held dear. How did you deal with it? I remember for myself one big attachment that I had as a young man. I wanted to become a professional freestyle skier, but because of a serious knee injury, I had to stop. The loss of that dream made me depressed for several years and I felt as if I'd lost myself. I spent most of my days glorifying the past and thinking about my peers who were now flourishing in the sport. For the first time, I experienced real jealousy. Other people had something that I wanted but couldn't get. This caused me a lot of suffering, so looking back, I can clearly see that it was my ego that had too much control. I would have felt less pain if I'd not been so immersed in my identification with this sport.

Now, are all forms of identification bad for us? The easiest answer to this question is that if one has not created distance between themselves and a strong identification, then it is potentially harmful. In other words, if they are not aware that there is a strong identification, one must be prepared to experience a lot of pain if this thing were to disappear from their life. Let's take elite athletes as an example. The Professional Players' Federation conducted a study 2013 which showed that 32 % of former sportsmen felt out of control in their lives for two years after quitting their career. A lot of them had problems with their finances, ongoing addictions and mental problems such as depression and anxiety.

The Constant Need for More

Have you ever worked towards a goal or looked forward to something and got it, only to ask the question of, is this all there is? Or what's next? If you really reflect on the question, I think you're guilty of this. At least I am, working towards goals is a part of my daily life. Even writing this book is a goal of mine. But what happens after?

Will I be complete once this book is? No, because I already am, and so are you.

Our egos will tell us that happiness is in the future. It will tell us that we simply have to climb this mountain first. That's one concept that we'll have to understand if we want to become a warrior of peace. We are not striving for completion. We accept that the world will not always be the way we want it to be. We accept that straight lines are rare in both life and in nature. The word "acceptance" holds more power that one might imagine. People often spend their time worrying about things that they can't control instead of changing things that they can. Let's accept the fact that our worries about the global economy won't get us far, but doing something about our personal finances will. Let's accept responsibility for being present with our kids while they are still young. Let's accept the present moment even though we might be going through hardships. Let's accept the present moment everywhere in our everyday life without glorifying the past or dreaming of a better future.

Chapter 5: Becoming More Mindful

Everyday

You can carry that experience of mindfulness with you throughout the day. You don't need to stop and meditate in order to be more mindful. Focusing your thoughts and attention on just one thing at a time and not sleepwalking through your day can change your entire life for the better. Once you start meditating you will notice that you automatically start becoming more present throughout the day. Cultivate that awareness and see how many other ways you can stay present during the day.

As Kate's story demonstrates most people don't even realize how much of their day is spent on auto-pilot. When was the last time you really were present during your entire day? Most people couldn't even say when the last time they felt really focused and alert was.

Here are some of the ways that you can practice mindfulness throughout your day:

Take a walk during lunch alone. Breathe the fresh air and notice the beauty of nature all around you.

Turn off your phone, computer and tablets by 9PM at night. Read a book, take a bath, or have a conversation with a friend or loved one.

Wake up 15 minutes early and meditate to start your day.

Set your alarm and wake up before dawn. Make a hot cup of tea or coffee and go outside to watch the sunrise. Take the TV out of your bedroom. Turn your bedroom into a sanctuary of quiet and relaxation.

Before you turn on the TV ask yourself if you really want to watch something or if it's just a habit. If it's just a habit don't turn it on.

Write a letter to a friend. Using pen and paper, not email. Send it.

Be creative. Creativity is playtime for your mind. Get your paints, buy a coloring book, buy some soft yarn and make yourself something. Whatever artistic pursuit you enjoy it do it more often.

Eat breakfast and really taste it. Don't just shovel food into your mouth.

Exercise. Everyday. Try yoga, join a sports league, try new activities that will get you off the treadmill and interacting with the world around you.

Managing Stress and Anxiety with Mindful Meditation

Stress can damage your physical and emotional health in a huge range of ways. Over the last decade doctors have found out that the effects of stress are far worse than was previously though. One of the reasons why stress is so damaging is that we live with so much of it.

Stress and Your Health

The fast pace of modern life combined with the pressure to always be connected, to work longer hours and to work harder while maintaining relationships with family and friends and dealing with financial pressures and other stressors means that most people these days live their lives in a constant state of being stressed out.

When you are stressed out the adrenal glands go into overdrive pumping out adrenaline and cortisol, two hormones that are necessary to survival but can damage the body over time.

When you are in a stressful situation your body goes into "fight or flight" mode as your brain and body try to figure out how to deal with the threat. Adrenaline and cortisol are pumped through your body to give you the extra strength that you need. They are supposed to be a short term solution to a big problem.

But when you're constantly stressed out and your body is constantly flooded with those two hormones your body gets ravaged by the effects of being in a perpetual "fight or flight" state. It can take hours for the effects of the adrenaline and cortisol to wear off. When you are in state of stress day after day for long periods of time those powerful hormones can ravage your body.

Take a look at some of the ways that stress can cause illness. Some of them you probably know but others might be a surprise. In addition to things like heart disease and hypertension stress can cause:

Heart attacks

Irregular heartbeat

Panic attacks

Back aches

Headaches

Body aches

Heartburn

Stomach aches

Infertility

Irregular menstrual cycles Insomnia

Depression

Anxiety

Auto-immune disorders

Neuroscientists from the University of California Berkley performed a ground breaking series of experiments showing that not only does stress damage your body it can actually rewire your brain.

The study, which was done as part of a series of tests seeking to show a correlation between kids who are exposed to high stress situations as young children with increased risk of mental illness in later life, showed that high levels of cortisol that were present in the body for long periods of time actually can damage the brain and rewire parts of the brain.

Clearly, stress is more dangerous than most people realize. It's so common to have to juggle so many things these days that people don't even think about how much stress they are exposed to every single day.

Mindful Meditation and Stress

Mindful meditation is one of the most effective ways to get all that stress under control and keep it from damaging your brain and your body. Protecting your long term health and eliminating anxiety is really as simple as learning to practice Mindful Meditation. Let's take a look at some common stressors that most people deal with every day and see how Mindful Meditation can help alleviate that stress.

Once you start looking for ways to incorporate mindfulness into your day you will see opportunities to use Mindful Meditation in situations that affect your life each day.

Mindful Meditation for Seniors and Retired People

Seniors or retired people may be dealing with a unique set of stressors related to aging, retirement, and dealing with a major life change. When you have spent many years working and retire it's easy to feel lost or feel like you no longer have a sense of purpose.

Mindful meditation and learning to focus on being present in the moment can alleviate that stress and give you the mental clarity that you need to enjoy this stage of your life. By learning to be comfortable in each moment as it comes you will be able to enjoy the freedom that you now have to pursue any activities or goals that you have been putting off for years.

Meditation and Loneliness

Once you retire you may also start to feel lonely without the familiar faces and interactions that you used to have every day. Talking with co-workers and clients, going out for meals or just running errands, and talking to friends and family help us stay connected to the world. When you are no longer working you may find yourself alone a lot more.

Mindful meditation can help you deal with that loneliness by helping you focus on what is around you right in the present moment instead of thinking about the past or feeling anxiety about the future. A few minutes of meditation can give you the perspective that you need to keep a healthy attitude about retirement and aging.

Mindful Meditation for Young Adults

Seniors and those who are retired aren't the only ones who can suffer from the unique stress and anxiety that comes from major life changes. Young adults who are entering the workforce or entering college can also feel lost and lonely and uncertain about the direction of their lives. Mindful meditation and focusing on just the present moment can have the same benefits for young adults that it has for seniors and retired people.

Young adults may have a harder time dealing with the anxiety and stress of going out on their own because it's the first time that they've faced adult responsibilities at the same time that they are facing situations like peer pressure and the pressure to succeed and not make any mistakes. Because many parents have placed high expectations on their children the young adults may be dealing with excessive pressure to succeed right out of the starting gate.

Developing a regular meditation practice can help young adults manage the stress of becoming adults by teaching them how trust their own instincts and accept responsibility as well as teaching them how to take care of themselves. By learning meditation and mindfulness now, young adults can set themselves up for a lifetime of good health and less anxiety and stress.

Chapter 6: Taking The Mystery Out Of Meditation

To understand why there has been such a surge in the practice of meditation in recent years, it's probably best to first begin with a quick outline of its history and origin. Despite the fact that an exact date for the advent of meditation is unknown, archaeologists and scholars alike put a date for the first possible link to meditation at about 5,000 years ago. Although hard to prove, researchers believe it's also possible that even primitive hunter-gatherer's may have meditated while staring at the flames of their fires. After all, fixating on an object is often customary in many forms of meditation.

Beyond that, the first recorded histories resulted from the teaching of the Vedas, found in the Indus Valley, an ancient civilization located today in Pakistan and northwest India. Then, about 600-500 BC, meditation was thought to take root in Taoist China and Buddhist India. Between 400 BC and 200 AD, the Bhagavad Gita, often referred to as the Gita, was written. The Gita is a Hindu poem that discusses the philosophy of meditation and how people are to rise up and live a spiritual life. In 653 AD, the first meditation studio opened in Japan. Japanese Buddhism evolved later in the eighth century.

Fast forward to 1922 when Hermann Hesse published Siddhartha, the story of Buddha's journey of self-discovery. The **Tibetan Book of the Dead**, a book of Tibetan Buddhism, was published in 1927. In the early 1950s, the Vipassana Movement, often call the Insight Meditation Movement, began in Burma. Origins of this movement can be found in the traditions of Laos, Thailand and Sri Lanka. In the 1960s, Hatha Yoga and Transcendental Meditation gained enormous popularity in America and in Europe as people celebrated experimentation.

In 1979, The University of Massachusetts started a meditation-based, stress reduction program to treat patients with chronic illnesses and anxiety. From this program, an interest of mindfulness practices and meditation grew dramatically in the medical community. With this advancement, doctors and scientists are even now identifying differences among the various meditation practices and employing their benefits to treat their patients. This is often referred to as alternative medicine and consists of a wide variety of health care practices and therapies.

Between 1996 and 2003, many outreach centers began and books were published about meditation, meaning to introduce people to this new "source of healing". Then in 2007, a study published by the National Center for Complementary and Alternative Medicine, showed that more than 9% of Americans now meditated. **2** That's millions of people, worldwide.

Today, there are more meditation groups, clinics, yoga classes, wellness programs, retreats, spiritual centers, and individuals practicing meditation than at any other time in history.

Still, even in the most enlightened society, meditation is still a mystery to many people around the world. Not surprisingly, people and societies with little knowledge of meditation practices continue to refer to meditation as something akin to an out-of-body experience. After all, so little is known about the mind, its powers, and its functions. This makes it difficult for an individual to distinguish between, say, self-hypnosis and the real process of mental well-being, known as meditation. Studies are now only beginning to reveal the effects, as well as the many benefits of meditation on our minds and bodies.

Although many people associate meditation with eastern religions, meditation also plays an internal part in many other religions, including Judaism and Christianity, as well as Hinduism, Buddhism and Islam. While each religion practices meditation in the same essential way, each faith draws on its own stories and teachings.

Hindu meditation is often defined as a state of relaxed contemplation, or state of reflection on the present moment. The goals of Hindu meditation include spiritual enlightenment and the transformation of attitudes; a journey to a deeper part of one's being. Buddhist meditation ascribes to core meditation techniques, such as Mindfulness of Breathing and Loving-kindness meditation. Each practice taught by the Buddha is designed to expand and evolve into a particular state or overcome a particular problem. Islam meditation is meant to open and strengthen a connection between God and his people. This is done through reciting the Qur'an.

Most Jewish people have never heard of Jewish meditation, yet some believe that meditation is essential for healthy Jewish living. Meditation experiences are widely found in the Torah, a Jewish sacred text. In much the same way, many Christian churches teach that through prayer, meditation becomes one very vital element in increasing one's knowledge of Christ. It aims to heighten a personal relationship with Christ, based on the love of God.

Meditation—An Under-used Tool for Managing Life

So, what exactly is meditation?

The exact definition of meditation is a bit unclear, and can vary depending on religious, cultural or pre-disposed beliefs. In essence, The Collins English Dictionary describes meditation as: "the practice of engaging the mind in contemplation or reflection." **3** In other words, engaging in mental exercise, such as concentrating on breathing, focusing on a particular thought, or reflecting on a specific difficulty or blessing for the purpose of healing and/or calming emotional, physical, and mental stress.

The term meditation refers to a wide variety of practices that are often used to help calm the mind. Meditation promotes concentration and can help a person feel more connected and happier; to appreciate life and the people around us. When practiced correctly, it can help to soothe many mental and physical health concerns, such as anxiety, everyday stress, fatigue, depression, and even high blood pressure. Practicing meditation can decrease pain from a nagging migraine headaches and muscle and joint problems. It can help the insomniac get a good night's sleep, is shown to improve brain function, mood, and can strengthen the immune system. That said, pinpointing the exact reason for that knot in your stomach, or the crushing pain in your chest, or why you can't get beyond a certain fear or break a nasty habit, can be tricky and not always obvious. Instead of facing these challenges, we often choose to procrastinate and move on, or ignore the problem. These are typical ways to cope. In fact, people do it all the time. But (spoiler alert) avoiding the symptoms can have lasting negative effects on your physical and mental health. That's why meditation is practiced an enjoyed by so many.

In essence, meditation is all about understanding what part the mind plays in managing how we deal with a health or mental issue, and discovering how to find a calmer, clearer and less oppressive outlook on life. Commonly, when practicing meditation, a person will sit quietly in a comfortable position, and have a limited focus of attention, such as concentrating on a specific breathing technique, the flame from a candle, or an object on the wall. This allows our attention to be focused on only one thing, without becoming worried about what is going on around us, such as noise from the television, or an outside distraction.

Learning to meditate and appreciating its many benefits can help us "step away" from fearful thoughts, negative images, physical tensions, and daily anxiety, to become a quiet onlooker of specific thoughts and emotions, as though watching them through a window. It can dramatically increase a person's ability to control fearful thinking, anxiety, panic attacks, and the like, by understanding new ways to respond to many predisposed thoughts and emotions. What's more, you don't have to be an expert meditator to reap its benefits. Practicing meditation techniques only once or twice a week during non-anxious periods can help quiet the mind and relax tense muscles. It will help control panic before it's too late, and decelerate anxiety before it has gained a solid foothold. In fact, setting aside a few minutes a day to meditate is good. But when you're stressed out, then a full hour or two is better.

While meditation is not yet considered mainstream, and is not always defined in a clear or concise way, one thing is very clear, meditation continues to be an underused tool for managing stress and anxiety, and that's unfortunate. Even so, the many thousands of people who are practicing meditation are enjoying the rewards of relief and relaxation from everyday stress and worry that meditation provides.

Chapter 7: Understanding Mindfulness Meditation

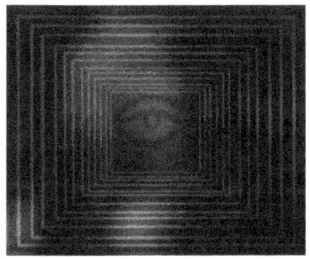

While it has been a part of the Buddhist faith for more than two thousand years, mindfulness meditation has become exceedingly popular in the Western world over the past several decades thanks to its proven ability to improve mental health including the treatment of stress, anxiety and even drug addiction. Professor Jon Kabat-Zinn brought the process to the attention of the modern world in the 1970s by publishing findings that linked it to stress reduction. This, in turn, lead to a flurry of new interest in the practice and a new understanding of the myriad of different ways that being mindful can help improve one's health by directly combating numerous different ailments. Studies on the topic have even proven so conclusive that it is now common to see mindfulness meditation being practiced everywhere from hospitals to prisons to veteran associations. Since its inception, mindfulness meditation been proven via scientific study to improve the physical wellbeing of those that practice it on a regular basis. At its heart, mindfulness meditation is all about focusing your mind to ensure that you are as fully aware of each moment as fully as possible. This, in turn, allows you to exist more completely in any given moment by expanding your consciousness to the fullest.

While it might sound like a tall order at first, the truth of the matter is that being mindful is a skill which means it can be improved by regular practice in much the same way as any other skill. Luckily, practicing mindfulness meditation is as easy as finding a few moments to focus solely on the present and the information that your senses are providing you in the moment. In fact, if you can find just fifteen minutes a day to practice, you will soon find that your overall stress is likely to decrease and your sense of self is likely to be at an all-time high. This isn't just an ephemeral feeling either, neuroimaging performed on those who practice mindfulness meditation on a regular basis shows that their minds actually process information more effectively, they are able to more easily regulate their emotions and their attention spans than those who do not make the practice a part of their daily routine.

Furthermore, the sooner you begin practicing mindfulness meditation, the greater the chance that doing so will ensure your brain retains more volume as you age, dramatically improving overall brain health as a result. This increased vitality also reaches the hippocampus which, in turn, makes it easier to learn and retain new information with minimal effort. At the same time, the amygdala becomes less active which means that the amount of fear, stress and anxiety that you experience will be decreased as well. Additionally, a daily dose of mindfulness meditation is enough to reduce the amount of cortisol, a hormone that increases stress levels, that the body naturally produces.

In addition to the physical changes that you are likely to experience when meditating regularly, regularly practicing mindfulness meditation will also help you to more easily free your mind from any negative thought patterns you might otherwise find yourself getting stuck on making it easier to focus on the positive instead. Mindfulness meditation is so effective at this task that a recent study out of Johns Hopkins University actually found that it is just as effective at treating anxiety, depression and attention deficit disorder as many of the leading medications specifically designed to do the same thing. Another recent study also showed students preparing to take the Graduate Records Examination, the most common test to obtain admission into graduate school, who practiced mindfulness meditation regularly prior to testing scored approximately 10 percent better than their less mindful peers.

With so many physical and mental benefits, is it any wonder that mindfulness meditation is revered by Buddhists all around the world? The practice has its roots in a type of structured meditation called vipassana which, when translated, refers to a mental state that promotes living in the moment while still being aware of how the present and the future intertwine. Those who master vipassana are said to more fully understand the universe as a whole as well as their place in it.

In order to reach a state of vipassana, practitioners strive for what are known as the three marks of existence: impermanence, non-self and dissatisfaction, which together are believed to bring unity to all living things.

Non-self refers to the idea of understanding the boundaries between the self and the physical world with the understanding that coming to terms with these boundaries make it easier to fully grasp the intricacies of both. Meanwhile, dissatisfaction refers to the innate desire seek satisfaction from fleeting experiences and the inevitable feeling that losing these things creates. This leads into the idea of importance as only by accepting the temporary nature of life can true happiness and inner peace be found.

Other reasons to practice mindfulness meditation

Mindfulness meditation naturally leads to a deeper understanding of the self and allows many people to take stock of their strengths and weaknesses, leading to personal growth.

Studies show that those who practice mindfulness regularly have a stronger memory, leading to an easier retention of facts in both the long and the short term.

In addition to the specifics, mindfulness meditation improves overall physical wellbeing with those who practice regularly reporting fewer instances of illness and a more rapid recovery when they do fall ill.

Mindfulness meditation can help improve emotional control while at the same time increasing one's threshold for pain.

As surprising as it might seem, making a habit of being mindful can actually make even the most middling music seem more engaging. This deeper level of engagement leads to a general increase of enjoyment, regardless of the type of music or any previous musical preferences.

With a regular dose of mindfulness meditation, many people experience a dramatic increase in their ability to empathize with others no matter what the situation. Furthermore, it allows practitioners to listen to other viewpoints more actively, more compassionately and results in their ability to withhold judgement on thoughts and ideas that differ from their own.

Chapter 8: What Is Mindfulness?

Mindfulness is an intentional acceptance as well as focus on ones emotions, thoughts, and sensations that are occurring in the present moment. In other words, mindfulness is focusing on the now and accepting it.

Have you ever met a person who just kind of floats through life with no worries, things just seem to fall into place for them and they don't stress about what will happen? These people are naturally born with the ability to focus on what is going on in the moment, but this can be learned.

Mindfulness means that you are paying attention on purpose. You have to purposely be mindful of what you are doing. For example, you may be aware that you are eating, you know that you are putting food in your mouth, but are you being mindful of what you are doing?

Let's look at this a little deeper. When we are mindful of our eating, we are able to notice all of the sensations that occur while we are eating. We notice our body's response to these sensations. We are purposely aware of the process of eating and if our mind begins to wander, we are able to bring it back to the eating process.

When we are not mindful of our eating, we may be eating while we watch television, we may be having a conversation, or even reading a book. When we are not mindful of our eating, a very small amount of our attention goes to the eating process. Often when this happens, we don't realize how much we have eaten or we finish the meal and don't remember eating.

If we are not mindful, focusing on what we are taking part of in the moment, our minds will wander without purpose. Most of the thoughts you will have will either be about the past or the future.

What you need to remember is the past is over and the future may never come. When we allow our minds to wander like this we reinforce the emotions that come with them, which causes us to suffer.

Let me explain it to you like this. If we sit and allow our mind to wander with no purpose, we may end up thinking about all of the bills that we have to pay. Then we begin to get upset because we don't know if we will be able to afford those bills. We may become depressed and guess what happens? We are not able to get the work done to pay the bills.

Or you allow your mind to wander and it goes back to some past event that caused you a lot of trauma. You begin reliving it and instead of focusing on the now, you begin to live in the past.

This happens more often than many people would like to admit. Let's take worrying about our bills for example. It may not cause you to not be able to get your work done, but it will cause stress in your life. It will take time out of your life that you could be focusing toward something more important.

The truth is that when we allow our minds to wander on their own, we seem to avoid thinking about the present moment the most. With mindfulness, we learn to only concern ourselves with what is going on right now.

This does not mean that we will never think about the past or the future. What it means is that when we do think about the past or future, we do so mindfully.

Mindfulness also means that we accept what is happening without passing judgment on the circumstance. Meaning that no matter what is going on, we do not get upset because things are not going the way you want them to go. Even if you are not having the experiences you want to have, you simply acknowledge that things are as they are.

In other words, it does not matter if the experience is unpleasant or pleasant, we treat the experience the same way. You see, we only want to acknowledge that yes this experience is happing, there is nothing that I can do to change it, and not spend our time focusing on it.

Chapter 9: Real World Mindfulness

By the time you reach the end of the three week plan, you should be noticing a meaningful reduction in your levels of stress. The practice of mindfulness can totally revolutionize the way you live your life if you let it. It can't make stress disappear, but it can help you react it to it in a healthy and healing way. One of the best ways this idea has been explained is if you imagine yourself on top of the ocean, the storm waves representing the stressors in your life bashing you left and right. With the mindfulness habit, you are placing yourself at the bottom of the ocean where the ocean's waves have little effect on you.

Using Mindfulness to Change Your Life

Now that you are comfortable with the idea of mindfulness and know some simple techniques, you can expand your mindfulness practice to other parts of your life.

Work

Work is a source of stress and anxiety for many people so it is the perfect place to practice mindfulness. It may be impossible to meditate at work, but that doesn't mean you can't incorporate the techniques you have learned into your workday. One method is to actively listen to your co-workers. Many of us, when we are having a conversation, spend our time thinking about what we will say next instead of paying attention to what the other people in the room are saying. If you catch yourself doing that, stop and gently bring your mind into the present moment. Really listen to what your colleagues are saying. If the conversation is stressful, practice your favorite breathing technique.

Mindful breathing is very useful for many work situations. It can help keep you from responding angrily during a tense phone call with a client, keep your tone even when public speaking, or calm when engaged in workplace conflict.

Play

Adults need to play as much as children do. If you find that you do not have room in your life for play, mindfulness can help you make room. One great way to practice mindfulness is to use it when you are with your children. Children are much better at staying in the present moment than adults are; they are curious about things adults take for granted. Take time to spot shapes in the clouds, build with blocks, or observe bugs in the garden. You can do these things even if you do not have children. Play is a wonderful stress reliever for people of all ages, and mindful play is especially beneficial.

Relationships

Personal relationships of any kind can benefit from mindfulness. Just as we often spend more time thinking about ourselves than we do our co-workers, we do the same in our personal lives. We do not really listen to what people say.

Mindful listening is a very good relationship skill to have. It can take practice to use it well, especially in troubled or contentious relationships, but it can completely transform the way you interact with other people. The next time you are talking to a friend or family member, center yourself with some mindful breathing and commit to listening carefully. Use the same gentle techniques you used during meditation to bring your mind back to the present moment if it wanders. The more mindfully you listen to the people in your life, the stronger your relationships with them will become.

Diet

When you make the decision to eat mindfully, it becomes easy to pay attention to the signals your body sends out when it is satisfied. Eating on the run often means that we bolt down food, only to feel overstuffed and sick when we are done. When you eat slowly and mindfully, chewing each bite, you will realize when you are full and stop eating.

You can also use mindfulness to help keep you from eating when you are not really hungry. A lot of us head to the refrigerator when we feel anxious. If you are mindful about it, you can stop and ask yourself if you are really hungry. If you are feeling stress or something other than hunger, you can try some mindful breathing and drink a glass of water instead of eating.

When you include mindfulness into all aspects of their life, you will see a positive transformation in your work, your home life, your body, and your mind.

Chapter 10: Putting Mindfulness Meditation Into Practice

Well, we have made it to the final chapter, where you can see what some of the meditations practiced in mindfulness look like. These meditations are simple and can be practiced as often as you require them to remain in a Beginner's Mindset.

Mindful Breathing

What to do:

Find a comfortable place to sit or lay down, although you can stand if necessary

Focus your attention on your breath, inhaling and exhaling.

Close your eyes

Take a deep inhale through your nose and hold it for a few seconds

Exhale slowly through your mouth

Repeat as necessary

A variation on this can be to just focus on your breathing, instead of using the exaggerated breaths.

Pay attention to the rise and fall of your chest and your stomach.

Let your breaths come naturally, whether that is slow, fast, deep, or shallow.

The point is to focus the mind inward.

If your mind wanders, this is fine. Just try to bring it back to the present, focusing on your breathing

Mindful Eating

What to do:

Slow down, and give your body a chance to give your brain the signals that it is full. The reason people tend to overeat is that your stomach does not send the signal it is full as quickly as the brain deciphers that you are still hungry. This is why overeating is so easy

Recognize what your hunger signs are. Are you hungry or are you responding to an emotional want? In a mindfulness practice of eating, listen to your body. If your stomach is growling, you are hungry. All too often the brain tells us to eat when we are not truly hungry. Mindful eating will help you to learn your body's signs of hunger.

Eat in a healthy environment. Try not to eat alone, or wander around looking for snacks, where you are more likely to overeat and binge, but set certain times and places to eat. This simple act of making a meal and sitting at the table, especially with other people, can rewire your brain to know when it is hungry or not.

Eat healthy foods, not foods that are comforting. Choose foods that benefit you nutritionally, not emotionally. As you practice mindful eating, it will become easier to start to think of healthier foods as comforting.

Think of where your food came from. It is easy to not think about where food comes from beyond the supermarket, but mindful eating means to consider that food, all the people who worked to create it, from a loved one who cooked it, to the people at the store who packed it, to the farmers and ranchers who grew and raised it. By slowing down and considering this, mindful eating will bring you a greater appreciation for the food you put into your mouth.

Mindful Sounds

What to do:

Have a chime, or bell nearby on a timer, where you are sitting or laying quietly. Ring it. As the bell fades, start to listen for the following:

Sounds in the background. Mindful hearing means letting yourself focus on those sounds that are always in the background, like a fan whirring, traffic noises, crickets. As you begin to notice them, let go and try not to identify them, but instead just take pleasure in hearing.

Sounds of melody. Music can arouse emotions which is why music is enjoyable. When you sit quietly, you will discover melodic sounds all around you. Birds, rain on the roof, a siren. When you practice mindfulness, try to find the emotional response to each of these sounds.

Sudden sounds. When a sudden sound interrupts us, it can shock us back into awareness. These shocking noises can wake you up and back into the present when you have been lulled into normal thought patterns.

As the ending bell fades, let that sound stay with you a moment. Then allow it to help you transition back to your day. Sounds are around you at all times, mindfulness and awareness teach to be open to them, and this one more way to appreciate the world around you.

Mindfulness of Emotion

When unpleasant emotions start to creep in, this exercise can help you to stop, refocus, and understand your current emotions.

Requires about 10 minutes, or longer

What to do:

When you start to feel an unpleasant emotion, stop, sit, take a deep breath, and then focus on the shame, guilt, anxiety, frustration, fear, or anger that is bothering you. Do not stop it. Just sit with it in an attitude of mindful openness and acceptance.

Pinpoint the Emotion; there could be several happening at the same time, scan your body for the strongest one at that moment.

Acknowledge the emotion is there. Say what it is you are feeling at the moment out loud.

Take several more deep breaths, then accept what it is. You do not need to deny these emotions have risen, instead accept it for what it is, be in the present, and say to yourself "I accept that I feel very angry right now.".

Open and embrace the emotion. Through acceptance, you can embrace the feeling in your awareness, which can be soothing and help you move on from the emotion faster. In this space, you learn that you are not your anger, fear, or embarrassment. You are bigger than that.

Realize that all Emotions are not permanent. They come, they stay for a while, and then they go away. Your job in mindfulness is to simply be aware that they are there, and accept you are feeling them.

Do not consider yourself in a negative light because you are experiencing these emotions. Mindfulness can help you to see these emotions as a mental event that is passing through, just like waves in the ocean coming in and receding on a beach

Figure out where emotion came from and then respond to it. Once you have calmed down from this emotion, look into yourself and try to investigate what may have brought on the emotion. Once you have identified the cause, you can reflect on it, embrace them, realize that it is what it is, and move on about your day.

Be open to the outcomes of your emotions. Denying them will only elevate them within you, and it will not give you the opportunity to examine them to see what your triggers are, and through that, you can program your brain to react differently the next time a similar situation arises.

Here is a quick version of the emotional acceptance exercise, one you write down and keep in your pocket if you need to:

Emotional Acceptance in 4 easy steps:

Observe: Become aware of the feelings in your body

Breathe: Take several deep breaths. Breathe in and out

Expand: Allow room for these emotions, create a space for them

Allow: Allow the emotions be there, do not shove them aside.

Mindfulness and Thoughts

One of the most common exercises taught for Mindfulness of Thoughts is called "Leaves in a Stream."

Takes about 10 minutes

Imagine you are sitting by a stream, with the water in front of you

Listen for any sounds from the water

Look for any trees around the stream

Look at the stream, are there any leaves from these trees floating in it

Now, as a thought enters your mind, acknowledge it, then put it onto one of those leaves floating in the stream

Watch the stream float away

Repeat this with every thought you have during the duration of the exercise

Once you acknowledge your thoughts, you do not need to keep them. You do not need to feel attached to these thoughts

Only acknowledge, then let it float away on a leaf

By allowing these thoughts to go away, it lessens the hold on you these thoughts have and their intensity.

By lessening them, you can clear the chatter in your mind, and be more mindful of the now, and aware of your body.

Another exercise to help you with thoughts and mindfulness is called RAIN, an acronym to help you remember how to practice mindfulness:

R: Recognize what is happening

A: Allow that experience to be there as it is

I: Investigate it with kindness

N: Natural awareness comes from not identifying with the current experience

Recognize: This means that you are acknowledging the thoughts and feelings within you. The first step to cleansing yourself of negative thoughts is to just recognize that they are there. Common negative feelings include fear, unworthiness, shame, anxiety, depression, and a critical inner voice. Everyone has a different response to each of these emotions, some stay very busy to avoid these feelings or prove to themselves they are valuable, others freeze because they are scared of failure. Still, others may develop addictive behaviors like alcohol, drugs, or overeating as a way to face their shame or fear. Whichever of these people you are more like, remember that it is unhealthy, and recognizing your emotions and thoughts can help you to slowly cleanse yourself of them.

Allowing: This means that your emotions, feelings, sensations, and thoughts are all recognized as just being there. People react to unpleasant experiences in three different ways, numbing yourself to the feeling, stacking up the judgment, or placing your attention somewhere else. None of these corrects the current experience, and they do not help your brain to react differently the next time something similar occurs. By allowing those thoughts or feelings to be there, you are honestly accepting and acknowledging the presence of them.

Investigate: This means that you are activating your curiosity, the yearning to want to find the truth, which can then direct your focus to your present moment. By pausing for a moment and asking yourself what is happening to me, you can begin to investigate these feelings. Unless you examine these feelings and thoughts and bring them out to be looked at further, these thoughts or feeling will always control how you react when a similar situation happens again

Natural loving awareness: This means that when identification of the smaller things is found, you can loosen yourself. The practice of non-identification helps us to become not stuck with any of your emotions, sensations, or stories. You can begin to live with openness and express your awareness. Loving awareness is a liberating feeling, the ability to function in a natural state of awareness. As you continue to practice mindfulness, you will begin to notice a change in how you see things, how you react to them, and how you can learn from these experiences the next time they arise.

Throughout your life, you have been conditioned to live within certain boundaries, certain expectations, certain uncertainties. It is the nature of the world around us with all of the craziness of school, work, relationships, and relaxations. The world would have you believe that you must own certain things to be happy, and how much of it you should have. Technology has become a daily way of life, and we find ourselves becoming more and more addicted to it. This can all play into the innate feelings of greed as well as the feelings of self-worth.

You have been conditioned to believe that you are worth more in other's eyes if you have a college degree, the newest cars, the newest phones, the best TV streaming abilities, and of course, how much money you make. Society expects you to put on a showy display, and through that, you have learned to find your feelings of fulfillment, self-worth, completeness, aliveness, intelligence, and love.

As we have discussed in this book, through the practice of Beginner's Mindset, practicing mindfulness, awareness, and following the exercises in this book, you can begin the process of slowly cleansing yourself of these preconditioned mindsets. Just because your environment says one thing, you have the power within you to change how you view it. You can harness the power of your brain and learn to be aware of your thoughts, your feelings, and the feelings and thoughts of those around you. Mindfulness will help you to understand all of these things, and allow you to live in the moment, instead of the future, or the past, dwelling on possible outcomes that do not pertain to you in the now. Every day presents its own stresses and anxieties, so live each day to its fullest, never worrying about yesterday's problems or tomorrows possibilities. Mindfulness and awareness will help you to stay present and focus on the most important things: you, what you are feeling now, what you are doing now, how you fix things now, and how you learn to prevent them now.

Chapter 11: Positive Impacts

Relationships, Love, and Happiness

Mindfulness practices have created many tested and proven positive impacts on relationships, love, and happiness. The benefits of bringing in mindfulness practice into your life seem to grow, expand, and reach out to every aspect of your existence. Practicing mindfulness does not only improve your well-being, it also creates positive impacts on your relationship, love life, and happiness respectively.

Relationship

A study at the University of North Carolina about non-distressed couples and relative happy couples that practices mindfulness shows that there were improvements and more happiness. Mindfulness practice is like a skill, a practice on compassion which you can incorporate into your relationship to enable you to have an available, easy way of calming yourself down whenever you are distressed. It is the method we can use to improve our awareness of our experiences and enables us to have the space to make our own choices in our day to day existence.

When you inculcate mindfulness practice into your life, you can now see how having this ability can improve and promote better results in your relationships. Mindfulness is the perfect key to maintain our emotional balance. It is the means that you can become aware of your thoughts and remain connected to your feelings without becoming a victim of intense and inappropriate reactions that come from our past unresolved issues.

Staying in a romantic relationship can be very complicated in so many ways. It can change the way you view yourself and your environment. A romantic relationship can make you a slave to the will of your partner before you know it. When you think of how you can get hurt in this state of vulnerability to your partner, you may become reactive which will lead to the risk of sabotaging your relationship yourself. You will become aware that you are acting in the best interests of your relationship.

Mindfulness practice is the only thing that can provide you with the valuable instrument to face the day to day challenges that comes from being close to your partner. It will provide you with calmness and focus that will allow you to bring out your problem in the open for discussion and settlement instead of embarking on a screaming match with your partner. Mindfulness practice will enable you to be more compassionate, open and self-aware.

It will take your focus away from the automatic pilot, judging thoughts, negativity and enable you to be more connected, and present to things that are happening before you. It is not a wrong analysis to say that people who practice mindfulness are better relationship partners. A research report on a Meta-analysis by the "Journal of Human Sciences and Extension" supports that higher rate of mindfulness practices results in more satisfying and happier relationships.

There are many ways that mindfulness can help your relationship.

They are as follows:

Mindfulness will enable you to be attentive and more present in your relationship

Remember how frustrating it can be if you are trying to talk to your partner, but he or she is busy sending texts, checking e-mails, or worrying about work. Mindfulness practice will help you to change back your focus which has fallen into the autopilot mode and directs it back to your partner. This allows promoting more love and intimacy that brings connection, and happiness in a relationship.

Mindfulness practice will reduce negative reactions

This practice regulates that part of the human brain that induces the fight, freeze and flight reaction from a person. It eliminates this reaction so that couples can come out of the emotional distancing or destructive arguments.

Mindfulness practice enhances emotional regulation

Through mindfulness, the prefrontal cortex which is the executive center of the brain sends a message to amygdala that is in-charge of promoting fight, freeze or flight to cool down that things are okay. This action will enable you to walk away or advice your partner to "Stop!"

Mindfulness practice improves self-awareness

Mindfulness will help us to notice when our actions are unhealthy to our relationship, remind us of our core values and redirect us to the way we want to act. This practice will pull you back from the impulse of manipulation and destruction that may arise in a relationship.

Mindfulness promotes compassion

Mindfulness practice changes the part of the brain that is related to compassion and empathy. This action can help you to understand your partner's emotions and perspective more to enable you to have empathy and compassion for them. Compassion is what will enable you to show your warmth and love to your partner who enhances intimacy. Mindfulness practice will show you the way instead of the avoidance mindset.

Love and Happiness

Love and happiness are not what happens to you like that; you have to choose to love and to be happy. If you incorporate mindfulness practice into your relationship, you are increasing your chances of love and happiness. According to positive psychology, you can improve your happiness if you can change the way you are aware of the world.

Research carried out over the past 20 years have shown that mindfulness practice can have a positive impact on love and happiness. What it involves is only to practice mindfulness for 15 minutes in a day and see the barriers holding your happiness and love begin to crumble. You will then begin to connect with your partner, spouse or children in a meaningful level.

Mindfulness will enable you to overcome that feeling of insecurity that is hindering you from becoming more open to trust, love and intimacy that promotes happiness. This practice is the best way to rewire your brain and to overcome those defenses that are not helpful to your love and happiness. When you drop the pain, suffering, hurt and barriers which you have accumulated over the years, you will be free to love and be happy.

When you are happy and feel loved, you will begin to enjoy the following benefits;

1. You will be in a position to manage your stress levels better

2. The risk of suffering from depression will reduce

3. The health of your heart will improve

4. You will have a longer lifespan

5. It will boost your self-esteem

Mental Clarity, Work efficiency and Coping with Stress

Mindfulness practice is a rare technique which is tested and proven to provide you with a mental clarity that will result in coping with stress and work efficiency. This result is due to a physical alteration that occurs in your brain during the time of mindfulness practice. According to researchers from British Columbia University, there are significant changes that exist in the eight regions of the brain especially in two regions during mindfulness practice. Mindfulness practice that you may think is a simple activity increases the brain tissue density and the brain activity.

It touches the following regions of the brain:

☐ The ACC was otherwise known as "anterior cingulate cortex." This part of the brain enables you to exercise self-control, resist distractions, avoid impulsiveness and to focus.

☐ The hippocampus- This particular region of the brain is in-charge of resilience during challenges and setbacks. It eliminates stress readily which makes it a must-have for most individuals.

If you can control these brain regions through mindfulness practice, you will no longer feel out of control, going from one thought to another and stop dwelling on negative thoughts. You can now cruise through your hectic day with calmness and productive manner. This is all thanks to mindfulness practice that maximizes your brain density where it is needed. This practice may seem complicated or abstract to carry out, but in reality, it is straightforward to accomplish.

All you have to do to gain mental clarity, work efficiency and coping with stress are the following:

Concentrate on your breathing

You can sit down on a comfortable seat while your feet are flat on the ground and focus your attention on your breathing. After some time, you will become used to the process and can learn how to immerse yourself in your breathing process. You will no longer remember any other thoughts whatsoever as you feel the air passing in and out of your body.

Go for a walk

You can also practice mindfulness during walking. All you have to do is to pay attention to every step you take. Allow yourself to feel the movements of your feet as it touches the ground. Also, feel the sensations in the environment like the hot sun, the barking of a dog in the distance and the cool breeze. Don't allow other thoughts to creep in but focus more on the feelings of walking. This action will refresh and alter the frame of your mind.

Be aware of your body sensations

Even if you are very busy, you can always make time to feel your body without stopping your work.

Repeat any positive thing you know about yourself often. The objective of mindfulness practice is to quench the density of thoughts that cross your mind again and again. You can then use it to send a positive message to your mind so that your mind will remain on track.

The techniques mentioned above when practiced for a few minutes daily can make a huge difference reducing your stress and calming your mind. They will provide you with better clarity, and you can view things in a different light. Mindfulness practice can enhance the activities of your brain which as a result can de-stress and improve your work efficiency.

Effective Communication and Focusing

Mindfulness practice can positively affect everything in your daily living that range from your health, work and relationships. It affects your communication skills, the way you focus, how you can control your feelings, your listening ability, how you make decisions, your priorities and how you can retain your energy level.

Mindfulness practice can have a positive impact on your communication skills. Communicating with other people is what we do daily, although at our own pace. However, when the pace of our life increases the communication channels also expands. We tend to lose focus while sending or responding to messages. We will then switch to autopilot and answer mindlessly which do not make for effective communication because it is detrimental to success. However, when you practice mindfulness, your mind, head, and thoughts will clear up. This action will enable you to engage fully in any conversation thereby making for effective communication.

Another thing that mindfulness practice has a positive impact on is your power of focus. When you are suffering under the weight of work compilation, you will find yourself trying to finish one task while unconsciously thinking of the next one. Your mind will keep on wandering, and distraction will set in.

However, it is the mindfulness practice that will enable you to come out of this hole which you find yourself in. Mindfulness practice will make you aware that you are distracted from your initial objective. It will also bring you back to the present moment so that you can focus and accomplish your set task.

Chapter 12: A Few More Mindfulness Practices

Mindful Cleaning

You can clean mindfully. Here is the practice:

When you are cleaning your house, make sure you are not just cleaning. While you are vacuuming the rug, you don't want your mind to be elsewhere by watching TV or thinking about what you are going to do next. Focus on the task at hand. If you are wiping, simply wipe, if you are sweeping, then simply sweep.

When cleaning, show gratitude for the people in your life. The showing gratitude will help you be more mindful in your cleaning because one of the reasons you are cleaning the house so that your loved ones can live in it as well.

Pay attention to your actions and thoughts. While you are focused on cleaning, there will be unwanted thoughts that will creep into your mind. Simply observe your off-putting thoughts and then return to the tasks at hand. If you are sweeping the floor, pay attention to the dust that you scoop out or the bristles in the broom.

The cleaning is not limited to simple things like scrubbing or mopping alone. You can use mindfulness while de-cluttering your entire house. Studies have shown that de-cluttered home leads to a de-cluttered mind. Organize your home mindfully, this habit will lower mental clutter.

Brushing your teeth

You can brush your teeth mindfully. The practice:

As you know the bathroom floor has a different feel to it than the rest of the house. When preparing for brushing, ensure that you are aware of your feet on the floor, the texture and temperature of the floor on the bottom of your feet.

Be mindful of the color and the smell of the toothpaste as you squeeze it from the tube onto your toothbrush. Notice the texture and the flavor of the toothpaste as it enters into your mouth.

As you brush, notice the movement of your arms as it moves while you brush. Be mindful of each and every tooth in your mouth and the sensation of the brush on the gums. As you rinse, be conscious of the feeling of hot/cold water in your mouth as you shift it around with your tongue to clean your mouth.

Be aware of any unwanted thoughts and feelings that might arise while you brush your teeth. Just observe the thought and gently return your attention to your breathing.

Showering for Mindfulness

Incorporate the benefits of mindfulness through your morning shower. Here is the practice:

Turn all the devices that can be a distraction. You don't want any distraction while you shower mindfully. Turn your TV, radio, and if needed, keep the phone off.

As soon as you step into the shower, be mindful of all the things that are a part of taking that shower. Be aware of the texture and temperature of the handle of the shower as you turn on the shower.

Focus the sound of the shower. Notice the difference between the sound when you are under the shower or when the water directly hits the floor.

Feel the sensation of the warm/cold water on your body. Observe how easily it glides over your skin. Absorb all the feelings and smells that are associated with shampoo, soap and even the shower itself, while you clean your body.

As always, be aware of any distracting thoughts and feeling that enter your mind. Thoroughly enjoy your shower.

Chapter 13: The Basics Of Mindful Living

Mindful living is a concept that most people are not familiar with. Although this may be the case, it is an idea that can easily be understood. This chapter will discuss about what you need to know about mindful living.

Components of Mindfulness

Mindful living is defined as focusing on oneself to be able to make better decisions, appreciate nature and also be more receptive to providing solution to your problems. To achieve mindfulness, it is important that you achieve the three components. Below are the three components of mindful living.

Purpose

When we are on autopilot, our attention is swept away by a series of interruptions thus we lose our focus as well as purpose in life. Mindfulness is all about knowing how to do conscious deliberation so that we can find the original intentions of our lives. With mindfulness, we are more awake and more aware of what makes us happy.

Living In the Present Moment

Mindfulness allows us to stay grounded in the present moment. By being in autopilot, we often think about unnecessary events in our lives such as the past and present. Mindful attention is all about being engaged in the present moment and accepting things as they unfold in front of our eyes.

Non-Judgmental

When we are in the state of mindfulness, we are aiming to pay attention to our experiences as they arise without labeling or judging them. It allows us to become more aware of our perceptions and emotions so that we do not get swept away by them. With this, we become less reactive to things that happen in our lives.

Two Practices of Mindfulness

Mindfulness has two types of practices. It is important to know these types of practices so that you will know which approach works best for you. Below are the types of practices to achieve peaceful mindfulness.

Formal Practice

This refers to meditation which is commonly practiced by deep breathing and sitting while the eyes are closed. Formal practice is often done among practitioners of Buddhism and Taoism. Moreover, people who also do yoga also practice this type of mindfulness.

Informal Practice

This refers to anything that you do in your daily life. You can do your chores mindfully. The thing is that any routine or activity can be made into mindfulness practice as long as you bring your full attention to what you do.

So which type of mindful practice should you do? It depends on your preference. If you have a lot of time, then formal practice is a good option but if you don't have enough time, then can opt for informal practice.

Benefits of Mindfulness

Mindfulness can bring a lot of benefits to oneself. This is the reason why mindfulness is now being taught in schools, hospitals and workplaces. Below are the benefits that you can get from living mindful lives.

Mindfulness can reduce stress as well as other destructive emotions. In fact, studies have shown that mindfulness can shrink the right pre-frontal cortex of the brain which is responsible for a lot of negative emotions like anger, fear and sadness.

Mindfulness can be used as an effective way to treat depression without using adjunct medicines.

It can help treat insomnia because it can help bring peace not only to the mind and also the body. By being mindful before bedtime, you can focus only on positive things thus allowing your mind to sleep faster.

It can be used as an effective way to manage pain. Pain management is easily treated with mindfulness. The thing is that you thinking too much of stress can produce dangerous hormones in the body. Mindfulness helps prevent the brain from producing stress hormones thus allowing you to manage your pain.

Mindfulness can help improve your memory as it allows you to improve your focus and attention. By being mindful, you will be able to think of solutions to pressing problems and also remember things in detail.

Mindfulness allows you to increase your confidence as well as emotional resilience. Since you are focused on yourself and your capacities, you will not easily envy other people.

It allows you to feel everything even unpleasant thoughts but lets you feel them safely and detached from all negativities. Mindfulness does not make you feel like an unfeeling jerk but it makes you more in control of your emotions.

The thing is that mindfulness can help transform your world from inside out. It is a daily practice that you need to observe if you want to maintain peace, fulfillment and the feeling of wholeness.

Uses of Mindfulness

Mindfulness is not only practiced by individuals to achieve peace but it is also used by groups and organizations to achieve their goals. Below are the concrete applications of mindfulness in society.

Therapy

Mindfulness is used as a powerful tool to enhance psychological health. Its efficacy has been proven in treating a wide variety of clinical disorders such as anxiety, depression, OCD, PTSD, borderline disorder and substance abuse. Researchers indicate the patients who have underwent mindfulness as part of their therapy treatment were very receptive and showed higher chances of improvement.

Coaching

Mindfulness is a very important topic in coaching and experts have now been using this technique to improve the performance, reduce stress and improve the emotional intelligence of individuals. Moreover, it is also used in improving satisfaction and developing leadership skills among participants.

Employee Training

Many businesses use mindfulness to train their employees to perform better on their tasks. Employees can benefit from mindfulness by increasing their self-awareness, reducing self-influence on stressful feelings and to have better relationships with colleagues.

Chapter 14: Compassion For Self

"If your compassion does not include yourself, it is incomplete." - Buddha

You can't give what you don't have. Fill yourself with love, be kind to yourself, take care of yourself. Be full of love, full of compassion, full of joy so that you can give that to others. Don't be ashamed of being the greatest version of yourself. This doesn't mean being arrogant, but being kind and peaceful. It's okay to be full of yourself - full of love, joy and peace! Be very careful about what you fill yourself up with, because that will be what you offer to others. If you are full of anger, resentment, guilt, or shame, what can you possibly offer those you love?

You can't hide what's inside you, because that's what you pour out. If you don't have love and compassion in you, people will feel it. Even if you do 'nice' things for them, it will be tainted by the negativity you have inside.

Extending compassion to yourself is vital for well-being. Many people say they love others but they don't extend that love to themselves. If you are committed to creating a loving, peaceful world, you have to stop being abusive, unloving, and hateful towards yourself. Whatever energy you are generating, whether it's towards yourself or others, is making the world more loving or more hateful.

It's healing the world or creating more suffering in the world. Make a promise that you will create no more suffering and hate in this world. Extend the love and compassion to yourself.

Compassion for others

Compassion means understanding the another person's pain. Compassion doesn't mean 'being nice'. Sometimes the most compassionate action will generate hostility on the part of the other person because you are no longer enabling them. They won't like it. They may say you're being mean; you're not being nice. Compassionate action does not mean punishment. It comes from a place of deep care and concern for the person's well-being.

Sometimes our desire to be liked and accepted will lead us to do things that are not in the best interest of our loved ones. For example, the parent who allows their drug addicted child to live in their home. The parents provide food shelter and the child continues to feed his addiction. The parents will say, "I can't throw him out in the street!" The reality is if the child isn't given consequences, the addiction will end up killing him. The parent would rather have that than have the child mad at her or for others to think she's a bad mom for throwing her son out of the house. The most compassionate action would be to offer food and shelter while the child gets sober, but to not allow him to continue to use drugs while he lives in the home. If he does, he has to go.

If he is able to feel the consequences of his actions, this may motivate him to seek help. The parents must understand that it's his choice. They are only enabling him to kill himself if they let him stay and continue to use drugs.

What's often at the root of this decision is parental guilt, avoiding conflict, and fear of what others will think about them. Love says: I'm here for you, the door is open, but I won't help you destroy yourself. Stay true to yourself. Sometimes being compassionate means the other person won't get what they want. That is okay.

If you believe somebody cares about you, you can go a long way.

That is why it is so important to show your children and loved ones that you care. Don't assume they already know. Tell them and show them.

Manipulation masked as caring

Coming clean about manipulative behavior is vital for healthy relationships. People manipulate others in an attempt to have their desires fulfilled. You want your partner to be a certain way. You want your children to act a certain way. You don't want them to make you look bad. This means treating others as objects to be controlled and manipulated in order for them to serve the purposes we want them to serve. When you are trying to get something from someone, you're not able to recognize their humanity. That's a strong statement, but really, you are so focused on getting what you want that you're not thinking about what they want. You may totally disregard their thoughts and feelings. It makes true connection impossible. It's an isolating experience because true connection isn't possible when there's an agenda.

Have roles, but don't get trapped in those roles. The predicament of most parents is they get trapped in their role and they get trapped in seeing their child in the child's role. They get so caught up in making sure they are seen as 'good' parents, that they lose focus on the fact that the child has their own journey, their own thoughts and feelings. They compromise the relationship.

How to become someone people actually want to be around

Listen

Most people aren't being present during a conversation. They either have their attention elsewhere or are thinking about what they are going to say next. Stay quiet when someone is talking. Then, when the person is done speaking, wait a second before responding. They might not be done yet. This helps to assure that you are responding to what they said instead of what you were going to say . If you are thinking of a response while they are talking, then you aren't listening to them.

People subconsciously know when you are not listening to them. They may talk, but they won't feel heard. You don't have to agree with what they are saying, but the relationship will be strengthened because they feel heard.

Stop Complaining

Nobody wants to hear your complaints. Complaining comes from a context of powerlessness because it has no impact; it doesn't change anything. It just makes people annoyed with you. The reason people become so annoyed with complainers is because there's no empowered action behind the words, so the complaints persist. Complaining changes nothing; alters nothing.

Most people don't really get how useless complaining is. To get a sense of how much impact your complaints have on the world, sit in a room with an empty chair in front of you. Complain away. Tell the chair what you're upset about. Tell it how you feel about things, your opinions, what you like, what you don't like, what people should do, and what they shouldn't do.

Notice the response the chair has to your complaints.

Some people complain as if they expect the world to come to a screeching halt because they're upset about something. Life doesn't care that you're unhappy in your relationship. It just keeps going whether your relationships work or they don't work. And nobody cares that you don't like your boss. Life doesn't stop because something bad happened to you as a kid.

Life doesn't stop because your partner left you or because you got sick. Life will just keep going whether you're happy or not. It's up to you to take action to make it better, but complaining does nothing.

Become the Source of Solutions

In any given situation you can either be the source of problems (and complain about the problems), or you can be the source of solutions. If you are known as the source of solutions everyone will want to be around you. No one wants to be around people who are viewed as the source of problems or who just sit around complaining about problems. Wherever you go, be a solution. Be accountable.

Complaining reinforces the victim identity. You strengthen the victim identity by constantly talking about and thinking about how bad things are, how terrible your life is, how bad you've had it. It's fueling unhappiness, which drives people away.

Sometimes, you are impacted or directly affected by another person's hurtful behavior. Although you did not cause the pain, you are responsible for picking up the pieces and healing yourself. Your responsibility is to make conscious choices.

Be courageous enough to change it or fully accept the situation, but don't complain about it. Remaining in a helpless, complaining state has no impact and will never give you what you want. When you make conscious choices, you receive conscious consequences.

I'm not suggesting you always have to be happy about the situation. Everyone feels down sometimes. It's important to recognize when you're stuck in the negativity and have created an identity out of it. You have control over your life. You're not helpless.

When You Become Reactive

You're a human being and sometimes you're going to blow it. You'll say or do something in a moment in which you've lost touch with presence and have slipped back into your old patterns. Have Compassion for yourself. Instead of beating yourself up, just notice it and say "Oh, there it is again. I'm doing it again." Then just come back to the present moment.

On "Letting Go"

Sometimes we struggle with persistent thoughts about something painful that happened in the past. Well-meaning people will often advise us to just 'let it go'. If this gives you relief and you can just drop it, then great. But what happens when you can't let it go? Then on top of the thing that's distressing you, you start to feel bad about yourself. You think you're weak because others are able to 'let things go' and you can't. You think 'there must be something wrong with me because I can't let it go'. At this point, drop all attempts to let it go. There's no such thing as "letting it go" in your mind. What are you letting go of?

In these situations, letting go is just an idea that never happens. If you find yourself in the position of not being able to let something go, I would invite you to not let it go. Give up trying to let it go. Free yourself of that concept. Instead of moving away from it (let it go), turn towards the pain and begin to explore it. Move deeply into the exploration of the thing you can't let go of. What were the expectations you had? What are you hurt about? Acknowledge the pain instead of trying to 'let go' of the fact that there is pain.

As far as what to let go of, if there's any idea of retaliation or revenge, definitely let go of that.

Ways of letting go or avoiding ever getting to the place where you feel the need to let go:

Notice that you are here but you are wanting to be over there, whether that be in a physical space or emotional space. The pain comes from not wanting what actually is. You are still wanting to be in a relationship that no longer is: 'can't let go'. You are wanting what happened (somebody hurt you) to never have happened: 'can't let go'.

Freedom is wanting to be where you are. Begin to foster a sense of contentment with what actually is. Why? Because that's what *actually is.* Fighting with what actually is causes tremendous suffering and turmoil. The situation is probably painful enough as it is. You don't need to add to it. Learn to see what you can be at peace about in your current situation.

Making Right Choices

Every choice will either enhance your life or drain it.

When your life choices harm you, it's an indication that you've got to change course. Don't betray yourself by staying in situations that cause you harm. Betrayal of the self is the worst type of betrayal. It hurts when others betray us, but there's nothing worse than betraying yourself. How do you know if the situation is right? You feel energized. You might feel tired, but you don't feel drained or depleted. You feel at peace even when things are challenging. If you are not at ease or if you find yourself in a constant state of confusion, it is not for you. If something or someone is right for you, you won't feel like you have to compromise your integrity or change who you are in order to fit in.

Making requests

When you make a request ,remember that the other person has the freedom to say no. If you make a request with the expectation that the person will say yes, and then they say no, you get mad. All it means is that the other person never really had a choice. It means you're attempting to control the other person's behavior. If they don't do what you want, there will be consequences. If the other person doesn't really have the choice to say no, be honest about it from the start. Don't ask as if it is a request. That's manipulative. Clearly state what it is: an expectation.

A request is, "can you please take out the trash?"

The person has the freedom to say yes or no. A command is: "take out the trash, please". That indicates that there is an expectation that the person will do it.

Anger

Everybody feels angry sometimes. Anger is such an intense energy and many people were never taught how to manage it. Some people might think "I shouldn't feel angry". Don't judge yourself for feeling angry. If you feel angry, it means you're human. That's as far as it goes. Everything else is made up. You're not bad, or messed up or whatever your mind might be saying. You're just hurt and scared. It's your responsibility to heal, but don't judge yourself as defective because you feel angry. Many people are scared of their anger. It can be the most difficult emotion to regulate and many of us were never taught how to regulate it. Some of us explode and some of us hold it in. Lots of us have unresolved anger and we become explosive not because of the situation right in front of us, but because the situation activates some previous experience that's unresolved and that we feel really angry about.

Once you've resolved the past hurts that you're really angry about, you'll be able to respond to what's right in front of you, which is usually no big deal. If you are able to sense the anger coming, try to explain your anger instead of letting it build to the point you blow up. Sometimes the activation is too quick, and you're gone. The best thing to do at this point is to wait.

Don't say anything or do anything until the intense wave of anger subsides. This will usually only take a few minutes. Think of your mind as a snow globe, when you shake it (like when angry or excited), it's cloudy and you can't think clearly. But if you don't act, just be still and watch it settle, the intense energy dissipates and you're able to respond in a more productive way.

Once your executive functioning has returned, then you can explain your anger by stating that you feel anger because someone said or did something that you found hurtful or insensitive. "I feel angry that you didn't call to let me know you wouldn't be home in time for dinner. I waited until the food was cold. I felt disrespected." Then make a request: "From now on please call me to let me know not to wait for you." Once you have clearly communicated your request, it is up to the other person to honor the request or not. If they don't then the ball is back in your court. Will you drop your expectation that they call and let you know, accept that sometimes they won't call, or will you leave the situation?

Channel the energy of your anger towards something positive. Direct your anger towards what you care about, using that energy to impact positive change. Let it motivate you for good.

Honoring your truth

Pretending is for the movies. Real life requires the truth.

Trust yourself. When something is right, it will feel right. When something is wrong, it feels wrong. Don't allow anyone to disrespect you, manipulate you, or to treat you badly, whether it be your partner, your mother, your father, your sister, your brother, or your boss. You have the right to protect yourself and say no. If you don't feel like you can speak up because you are afraid of the consequences, think about how unhealthy that is. You have no voice in that relationship.

A healthy relationship allows for you to speak up and not be afraid that they will leave you, reject you, criticize you, abandon you, or hate you. If you self-censor for fear of their response, you are in an unhealthy relationship.

Practice: From this point forward, make a promise to yourself that you won't ever allow anyone to treat you badly, to manipulate you, to guilt you, or to disrespect you.

People might be better than you in some things but they are not more important than you. No one is more important than anyone else.

Beyond anxiety and depression

One of the most exciting discoveries of neuroscience is neuroplasticity - you can rewire your brain. You can create new neural connections and generate new thought patterns. Every single time you intercept a negative thought pattern, you are creating new neural connections.

Don't be discouraged when you blow it. Just recommit to intercepting the negative thoughts that keep you anxious and depressed.

Practice focusing attention on new thought patterns that support your well-being. You can become resilient and you can strengthen thought circuits that support resilience by doing continuous present moment awareness checks throughout the day, meditating, spending time in nature and becoming still as often as possible.

Talk therapy can be useful for processing your pain and weakening some of the stubborn negative thought patterns that make mindfulness so difficult sometimes.

Chapter 15: Mindfulness For Beginners

So, let me start again with a brief introduction on what mindfulness is, and then we will go on to the benefits of mindfulness, and the techniques of mindful practices. These three elements of mindfulness will be discussed in this chapter and the next.

What is Mindfulness?

It is the power and the ability of the mind to stay focused in the present moment without worrying about the past and/or the future. Mindfulness is a state of open and active attention on the present moment. Being mindful helps you focus on your thoughts, your feelings, and your sensations without forming any kind of judgment on them.

Without being mindful, we are actually letting life go by us. Being in an awakened state of mind is mindfulness. It is the ability not to dwell on what happened in the past and not to anticipate anything about the future. So, the synonyms of mindfulness can be awareness, focus, presence, attention, vigilance, etc. The opposite of mindfulness is not only mindlessness but also inattention, lack of focus, lack of engagement, and distractedness.

So, when you practice mindful meditation, you are focusing on a specific activity. So if you can start mindful breathing, you are focusing on your breathing such that the mind is made to be aware of everything that is happening when you breathe. Like this, every aspect of life can be done in a mindful way to ensure your mind is focused totally on the present moment.

The mind is very fleeting and it will keep leaping from thought to thought and it might seem like a gargantuan task in the beginning. The trick is in allowing your mind to go where it wants to, allow those thoughts to pass, and then, gently bring it back to the present moment. It takes time and effort and oodles of patience. But once mastered, you will find yourself leading a far more fulfilling life than before, irrespective of your beliefs, culture, or anything else.

Benefits of Practicing Mindfulness

The most common benefits of practicing mindfulness are those that help you lead your routine life in a more engaged and fulfilled way than before. Let us look at some of these common benefits if practicing mindfulness.

Mindfulness Decreases Stress and Anxiety

There are multiple studies conducted under the Mindfulness-Based Stress Reduction (MBSR) program, which revealed that mindfulness techniques play a very important role in reducing stress and anxiety. Moreover, there have been other studies, which also proved the advantages of mindfulness techniques to reduce stress in your life.

Mindfulness helps you manage your negative emotions effectively which, in turn, leads to decreased anxiety and stress. Let us look at the symptoms of stress and anxiety and then see how mindfulness helps to manage them. Symptoms of stress and anxiety include:

A persistent feeling of worry and anxiety

Getting easily irritated, agitated, and angered

Getting defensive and argumentative with people around you

Restless sleep

Waking up feeling tired and low levels of energy right through the day

A restless mind

Often critical of self and others

Difficulty in getting focus and concentration

Skin conditions and rashes that cannot be explained by any biological and/or physiological reasons

Grinding your teeth and/or clenching your jaws in the night while sleeping

Unexplained migraines and headaches

When you practice mindfulness and create a state of relaxation in your mind, the following benefits can be reaped:

Improved brain functioning

Improved immunity

Reduced heart rate and blood pressure

Improved focus and concentration

Increased sense of awareness

Clarity in thought and perception

Lowered levels of anxiety and stress

A feeling of calmness and relaxation

A sense of being connected with your inner self

All these will help you manage anxiety and stress easily.

Mindfulness helps you Manage Illness in a Better Way

The most studies groups in these regards are the cancer patients and those with chronic and/or terminal sickness. There have been many studies conducted in this realm which have revealed the following benefits of practicing mindfulness techniques:

Reduces stress symptoms

Enhances a sense of spirituality

Increases the ability to not reactive to negative emotions

Helps in overcoming traumatic experiences during treatments

Enhances vigor

Reduces fatigue

Yes, the symptoms may not really go away for these patients agonizing under the pain of terminal illnesses. However, practicing mindfulness does help them manage their illnesses in a much better way than without mindfulness in their lives.

People being treated for chronic back pain reported improved ability to manage their lives independently and also felt reduced pain with mindfulness techniques included in the treatment. These positivity creating techniques helped lung cancer patients become more tolerant of their difficulties, which resulted in improved care both for themselves and for their caregivers.

Mindfulness Helps in the Treatment of Depression

Mindfulness can be proven to be an effective technique to include in the treatment of depression. Mindfulness practice has found to be very useful in reducing symptoms of depression, stress, and anxiety and increasing compassion as compared to practicing yoga alone. The primary way in which practicing mindfulness helps in treating emotions is by helping the practitioner to manage emotions in a mature way.

Mindfulness techniques help practitioners step back from the emotions they are caught in and objectively view the situation which facilitated them to see suitable solutions to their depression-causing problems. Studies proved that in addition to imagery relaxation used to treat depression, teaching the patients a few mindfulness exercises improved their ability to cope with anxiety and stress much better than without the use of mindfulness techniques.

Mindfulness Helps in Improving Cognitive Abilities

Various studies conducted have proved the efficacy of mindfulness practice to improve cognitive abilities. Even short mindfulness training sessions are known to improve your brain's ability to process visuospatial aspects, helps in improving working memory, and the overall functioning of the brain.

Mindfulness techniques improve brain functioning by reducing distractions. Mindfulness techniques are designed to train practitioners to focus and concentrate on what they are doing at the current moment. When the entire focus is on the present moment, you will not be distracted by other fleeting thoughts that eat into your focusing capabilities.

Studies have proved that the brain cells function in such a way that they use specific waves or frequencies to regulate the flow of data just like how radio stations are designed to broadcast sound at particular frequencies. The alpha rhythm is one particularly active frequency and the cells in this frequency process the sensations of sound, touch and sight in the cortex, the brain's outermost layer.

These alpha frequency cells suppress distracting and irrelevant sensations such that the flow of sensory data between the regions of the brain happens smoothly and effectively. Practicing mindfulness techniques is known to help the brain adjust better and faster to the alpha rhythms so as to reduce distractions and improve focus and concentration.

Using Mindfulness to Manage Negative Emotions

Negative emotions are, perhaps, the biggest reasons for our high levels of anxiety and stress. Fear, pain, grief, embarrassment and other such negative emotions can wreak havoc in our lives. We have all been experiencing these emotions and continue to do so. If we can learn to manage these debilitating negative emotions, a large part of our stress and anxiety will disappear from our lives. Let us look at some of the ways we can handle and manage our negative emotions so that they do not overwhelm us with their power.

Stop and Turn towards the Emotion – Once you become aware of the negative emotion, you are feeling, stop for a moment, and turn your attention to the emotion. Take a deep breath and sit down and accept the negative emotion you are feeling, be it anger, resentment, embarrassment, stress, anxiety, or anything else.

Do not try to inhibit the emotion. Do not try to suppress it or ignore it. Most importantly, do not try to conquer it; at least not at this stage. Simply accompany the emotion you are feeling with a sense of curiosity and acceptance and without treating it with any kind of animosity or friendship. Simply be with the emotion.

Now, Identify the Emotion – Once, you have accepted the negative emotion, identify what you are feeling and give it a name. For example, if it is an embarrassment, you will know it and recognize it at this stage clearly and without ambiguity. In the previous stage, you are only aware that you are feeling something negative. Here, with a clear and calm sense of accepting the negativity, you will be able to clearly identify the negative emotion and be able to refer to it as anger, worry, sadness, or anything else.

Accept the Emotion – Again, let me take the example of being embarrassed. When you feel embarrassed, you do not need to be ashamed of it or deny the feeling. It is possible instead for your mind to accept and acknowledge the feeling. Say to yourself, "I accept the fact that I am feeling intensely embarrassed at this moment."

When you accept the emotion mindfully, you can hold it in your awareness and embrace it, which will make you feel calm and soothed. It is an act of showing compassion for yourself and a sense of responding to your own feeling of distress without hurting anyone else in the process. Accepting the negative feeling is much more effective than punishing yourself.

Open yourself to the negative emotion without suppressing it, ignoring it, or denying it. In fact, don't try to feel stronger than the emotion and challenge it. Opening up your mind and embracing the negative emotion effectively create you created a separate space for it to observe it without getting entangled in it.

By creating a separate space for the negative emotion, you will realize that you are not the anger or embarrassment or stress or anything else. You are larger than the emotion like how a mother who holds a crying baby is larger and more capable than the upset child. You are the mother and the negative emotion is your child. Embrace your child with compassion.

Know that Every Emotion is Impermanent - Soon, you will realize that all emotions are impermanent. They come, they rise to a peak, and they disappear. Like waves in the sea, they come and go. Your job is to teach your mind to patiently look at each wave (emotion), watch it reach its peak, and then watch it ebb away.

We are all conditioned to take all emotions, particularly negative ones, very personally. Mindfulness helps us understand that these negative emotions are only passing events in the mind; mere temporary waves that ebb and flow in the ocean of our awareness.

Investigate and Find Appropriate Responses – Now, that you have accepted that these emotions are impermanent and that they come and go, sit down and investigate as to why and how the emotion was triggered? Was it some thought? Was it a feeling of worry for something or someone? Was it some kind of comment made by a colleague, a friend, or a relative?

At this stage, you will realize that there are certain conditions based on which you expect others to behave towards you and similarly, how you behave towards others. These sets of values and beliefs and a reaction that was contrary to them could also have been the cause of your negative emotion arising.

Or it could have been a usual way of response to a usual event that keeps happening in your life. It could be anything. Simply allow your more awakened mind to find deep insights that seemed hidden hitherto because of the lack of awareness.

Once, you have understood the reason for the negative emotion and have seen it in the right perspective, you might want to respond to it or the people or the circumstances causing it in a way that could avoid the emotion to assail you again. Many times, mindfulness will teach you that there is really nothing to do except to learn to handle your own thoughts well and not take negative emotions seriously.

Finally, trust yourself in doing the right thing. To achieve this, love yourself first. Show self-compassion. Only when you love yourself will you find the wherewithal to love and show compassion to others around you.

Mindfulness is not only about managing emotions. It can also be practiced in your day to day routines including eating, conversing, exercising, walking, etc. The next chapter is focused on giving you some simple-to-follow techniques on how to practice mindfulness in your day to day activities.

Chapter 16: Living In The Present And Accepting Life Challenges

Hate the negativity that often surrounds you? Feel stressed or anxious? Overwhelmed by our hectic, fast-paced modern society? These issues are often the direct result of as vicious cycle known as "unconscious living". You can be unconscious about your lifestyle choices, habits, and thoughts. You can be unconscious about your true values, life priorities, and deeper longings. And you're unconscious about living in the present moment because you're preoccupied by past regrets and worries for the future.

Since you can never go back to the past and the future is yet to be here, both are futile. As such, both have no actual benefit to you. The only value the past has is a source of knowledge and experience, but because things are always shifting, even that information is not entirely stable. Neither can anyone foretell the future. Therefore, living in the present is a mentality which understands that both the past and the future are misconceptions. They are neither reliable or stable. Since you can only live the past in your memories and the future with your creative mind, they have no self-sufficient reality of themselves.

You cannot undo the past nor modify it, neither can anything you do now honestly creates the future. Holding on to the past does not change it, nor does fretting about the future shape it. The answer is to let both go and just live in the present. This very moment is the only thing you can have any charge over. Sadly, it's easier said than done, isn't it? The problem has to do with your imagination and your determination to practice mindfulness.

The ability to live in the present is not a theory, although there are many theories and even denominations dedicated to it. Since any skill is the effect of regular practice, living in the present is possible if you practice continually. The ability to practice something consistently, however, is only possible if you have a definite passion for something. Breaking free from being constantly tormented by feelings of guilt over something you did or did not do or never having to always be fearful about the future should be reason enough.

It is a troubling fact that most people have been accustomed to believe that living in the moment is improbable. There are too many things to do, too many things to expect for, too many things to learn, too many people to make happy, too many things to worry about, etc. Fortunately, it is possible to live in the present moment, and in this chapter, we will learn more about how to use mindfulness for a better you.

How to Let Go of The Past

There's a lot of people who have a difficult time letting go of the past, or whatever happened to them moments ago. Many people like to keep reminiscing the past. You can never go back to the past, but instead, you should always learn from it and make it grow you as a person. These past experiences can help you grow and mature. However, clasping to the past will strip you of the life that is happening right now. Thus, you need to fight your way to outgrow yourself from all the depressing and negative thoughts that your past experiences bring.

If your mind is motivated by fear, doubt, worry, negativity, and all other things that could prevent you from bettering yourself, you will face problems. When your thoughts are concentrated on the negative view of the past, you will lose perception of the joy of today. You will miss many possibilities present today because you are worried that things may happen the way in the past. Like the old saying, 'the past has a tendency to repeat itself.'

Do not let your mind dwell on your past experiences. You can prevent history from repeating itself, especially if you have already learned from it. Your mistakes are supposed to make you a better person since you already took away all the lessons from those experiences. Have faith in the present and the future. Leave everything behind, even your memories, whether good or bad. Do not let your past define you. You were given all the power to take control of your life; do not put that to waste. Always put your sight on what is happening today. When you do, you will get more out of life.

Make the decision to let it go.

Things don't fade away on their own. You need to be dedicated to letting go of the past. If you don't make this deliberate choice straight away, you could end up self-sabotaging any attempts to move on from this past hurt. To stop reliving the past, you will need to make a decision to let it all go. Making a choice to let it go also means accepting you have the decision to let it go.

Express your pain and your responsibility.

Express the pain that past experiences made you feel, whether it's straight to another person, or through getting it out of your system (like talking to someone, or writing in a journal, or writing a letter to someone). Remove it all out of your system at once. Doing so will also benefit your understanding of what specifically your pain is about.

We don't exist in a world of black and whites, even when sometimes it feels like we do. While you may not have had the same amount of blame for the hurt you experienced, there may have been a part of the hurt that you are also partially responsible for. What can you do the next time around? Are you enthusiastic about your own life, or just a cynical person? Will you let the past define who you are? Or do you understand that you are not your past?

Stop blaming others and acting the victim.

Being the victim feels safe - it's like being on the bright side of life in a world against you. But the truth is, the world largely doesn't care, so you need to get over yourself. Yes, you're special. Yes, your feelings matter. But don't get the idea that "your opinions matter and that your feelings should neglect everyone else." Your feelings are just one bit of life, which is all complicated and messy.

However, every day you have a choice, either to feel sorry about past pains or to feel good about them. Why would you let the people who hurt you in the past have such power? No amount of reflection has ever fixed a relationship problem. Never. Not in the entire history of the world. So why choose to engage in so much thought and devote so much energy to a person who you feel has done you wrong?

Focus on the present and the joy of today.

Now it's time to let go. Let go of the past, and stop celebrating it. Stop telling yourself that story where you are the forever the victim of regret and poor decisions. You cannot unravel the past, all you can do is get the most out of your day. When you focus on this very moment, you limit your time to reminisce about the past. When memories crawl into your consciousness (as they are forced to do from time to time), recognize them for a moment. And then bring yourself gently back to the present moment. Some people find it natural to do this with a conscious lead, such as saying to yourself, "It's all going to work out. That was the past, and now I'm concentrated on my happiness."

Remember, if we fill our brains and lives with hurt and negative feelings, there will be no place for anything positive. It's a decision you're making to continue to feel the pain, instead than welcoming happiness back into your life.

Conclusion

we are prone to rushing through our lives and not taking a step back to enjoy and appreciate what we have. This is the reason why there are so many people suffering from stress, anxiety and depression. Mindful living is something that all of us need so that we can face the hustle and bustle of life without losing ourselves in chaos. Mindful living can be challenging for many people but with the right guide, it can easily be done. Let this book serve as your guide so that you can start mindful living wherever you are. With this book, you will realize that anyone can do mindful living and enjoy the benefits of living a peaceful and calm life despite the many problems present in our environment.

www.ingramcontent.com/pod-product-compliance
Lightning Source LLC
Chambersburg PA
CBHW072014070526
44583CB00015B/1472